CHILDREN IN CRISIS

VIETNAM

The Boat People Search for a Home

Photos by John Isaac
Text by
Keith Greenberg

A B L A C K B I R C H P R E S S B O O K

W O O D B R I D G E C O N N E C T I C U T

Published by Blackbirch Press, Inc.
260 Amity Road
Woodbridge, CT 06525
©1997 Blackbirch Press, Inc.

First Edition

Printed in the United States of America

10 9 8 7 6 5 4 3 2 1

Photo credits on page 32

Library of Congress Cataloging-in-Publication Data

Isaac, John.
    Vietnam: the boat people search for a home/photos by John Isaac; text by Keith Greenberg.—1st ed.
        p.   cm. — (Children in crisis)
    Includes bibliographical references and index.
    Summary: A United Nations staff photographer presents an overview of Vietnam's history and his impressions of some of the people, particularly children, who have fled this war-torn country.
    ISBN 1-56711-188-2 (lib. bdg. : alk. paper)
           1. Refugees, Political—Vietnam—Juvenile literature.
2. Refugee children—Vietnam—Juvenile literature. [1. Refugees—Vietnam. 2. Vietnamese Conflict, 1961–1975—Refugees] I. Greenberg, Keith Elliot. II. Title. III. Series.
HV640.5.V5I73   1997
362.87'089'9593—dc20
                                      96-15394
                                          CIP
                                          AC

Opposite: A young Vietnamese girl waits for transport by boat to a refugee camp in Malaysia.

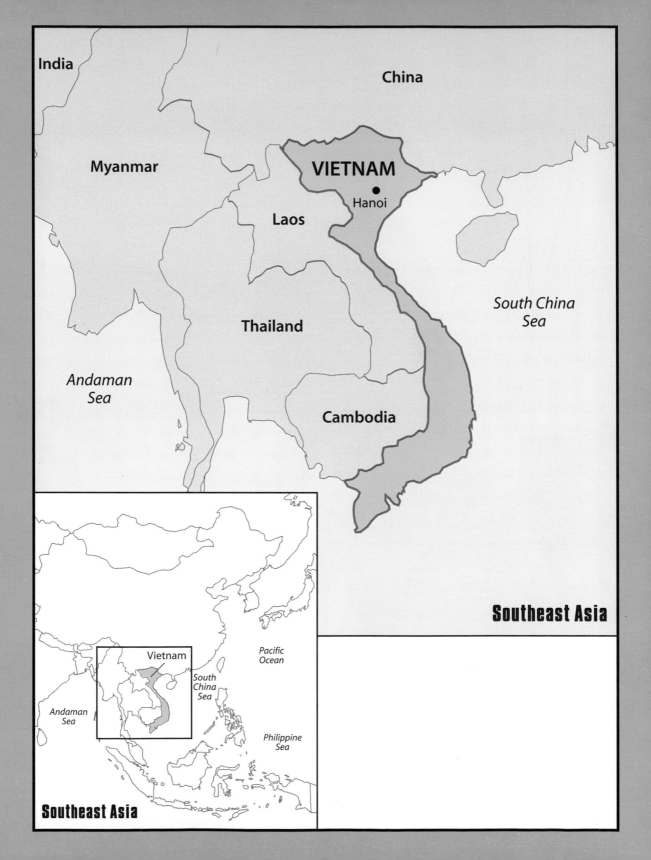

India

China

Myanmar

VIETNAM

Laos

Hanoi

Thailand

South China
Sea

Andaman
Sea

Cambodia

Southeast Asia

Vietnam

Pacific
Ocean

South
China
Sea

Andaman
Sea

Philippine
Sea

Southeast Asia

A LOOK AT VIETNAM

Vietnam is located in a part of the world called Southeast Asia, or Indochina. It is bordered on the north by China, on the west by the countries of Cambodia and Laos, and on the east and south by the South China Sea.

Vietnam is a long and narrow country. Its coast stretches 1,400 miles. Marshes, mountains, and tropical rainforests can be found in many parts of the country. Animals such as elephants, bears, tigers, leopards, and deer live there.

Today, there are nearly 72 million people in Vietnam. Most live in small villages. The capital city, Hanoi, is in the northern part of the country. It has 2.1 million people. Ho Chi Minh City—once called "Saigon"—in the southern section of Vietnam, has an even larger population, with 4.2 million residents.

Vietnamese is the main language of the country, but Chinese and French are also spoken. The

ancestors of the Vietnamese people were farmers. The Chinese invaded in 111 B.C., changing Vietnam forever. The Chinese influenced the Vietnamese language as well as the country's art, architecture, and music.

But the Vietnamese disliked foreign rule. During the 1,000 years that China controlled Vietnam, the people rebelled many times.

In the 1800s, France took control of Vietnam, though the people resisted. Then, during World War II, Japan invaded. Vietnamese leader Ho Chi Minh battled the invaders and fought them off. When the Japanese were finally driven out of Vietnam at the end of the war, the French tried to re-establish their authority.

Ho Chi Minh's forces fought the French, too. In 1954, the French surrendered, and Vietnam was split into North and South. Ho Chi Minh became president of North Vietnam. Its capital was Hanoi. The other section was called South Vietnam. Its capital was Saigon.

Ho Chi Minh worried leaders in the United States. He was supported by both China and the Soviet Union—Communist enemies of America at the time. Like his allies, Ho Chi Minh was a member of the Communist party. He wanted South Vietnam to unite with the North under Communist leadership.

Left: The streets of Vietnam's capital, Hanoi, are crowded with bicycles and motor scooters.
Inset: Ho Chi Minh was North Vietnam's Communist leader for many years.

In 1954, Communist fighters from the North—called Vietcong—were trying to take over the South. In response, American president Dwight D. Eisenhower sent military advisors to train the South Vietnamese Army. The next president, John F. Kennedy, also ordered U.S. troops to the country. Although the plan was for the Americans to simply help the South Vietnamese, the United States was slowly pulled into the conflict.

In August 1964, the Americans claimed that North Vietnamese torpedo boats had attacked two U.S. ships in Vietnam's Gulf of Tonkin. U.S. president Lyndon B. Johnson now ordered the bombing of military targets in North Vietnam.

President Lyndon Johnson visited U.S. troops in Vietnam in 1964.

By 1965, a total of 200,000 U.S. troops were in the region. They were assisting the South Vietnamese, along with soldiers from Australia, New Zealand, Thailand, South Korea, the Philippines, and other countries. In 1969, American forces in Vietnam reached 541,000, their highest number.

A total of 57,685 Americans were killed in Vietnam. An estimated 153,303 were wounded. Somehow, what started as a simple "advisory" role for America turned into a full-scale war. Meanwhile, more than 2 million Vietnamese on both sides were killed. Three million were wounded, and hundreds of thousands of children were orphaned.

This seemed to be a war without end. In the early 1970s, it spread from North and South Vietnam into the neighboring countries of Laos and Cambodia.

A Vietcong prisoner is held under heavy guard in 1968.

In March 1973, the Americans finally left. With the United States gone, the North Vietnamese were finally able to conquer the entire country. On April 30, 1975, South Vietnam's capital of Saigon was captured. It was renamed Ho Chi Minh City.

Thousands of flimsy boats—carrying hundreds of thousands of refugees—sailed from Vietnam after 1975.

In the turmoil of transition, about 500,000 Vietnamese refugees (people fleeing from political danger) tried to leave the country. They fled in rickety boats, hoping to find peace in some faraway place. As many as 75,000 of these "boat people" died at sea. Many who were rescued from ocean waters were placed in crowded camps in Indonesia, Thailand, Malaysia, the Philippines, and Hong Kong. There, these refugees waited for the United States, Canada, Australia, or some other country to take them in.

 # JOHN'S STORY

In 1979, the drama and tragedy of the boat people was international news. The United Nations (UN) sent workers to the camps to feed, clothe, and provide medicine for the hundreds of thousands of refugees. As official photographer for the UN, I also went along, taking pictures and witnessing the heartbreak and suffering as it unfolded.

The boat people who left Vietnam were not sure if they would survive their journey. For many of them, however, death while trying for freedom was better than death at the hands of the Communists. Many of the vessels were not strong enough to withstand the choppy waves and storms of the ocean. In the water, refugees drowned and were eaten by sharks. The boats that didn't sink were often packed and filthy. The boat people sometimes ran out of food, and starved while floating out to sea.

UN photographer John Isaac took this picture of Vietnamese children waiting aboard their crowded boat in Hong Kong harbor.

There were also attacks by pirates. These were people who lived normal lives during the day. But at night, they boarded boats and sailed out to the desperate refugees. The boat people sometimes thought they were about to be helped. Instead, boats were raided and burned. People were beaten, robbed, and sometimes murdered.

In August 1979, I visited the Songkla refugee camp in southern Thailand. It was there that I met a 13-year-old girl who survived a pirate attack. This poor child was scarred by memories she'd never forget. The pirates had attacked her mother and killed her father. The girl was one of only six people on the boat who lived through the horror.

The girl was sitting by the shoreline when I was introduced to her. She didn't look at me, and she didn't speak. All she did was stare out at the ocean.

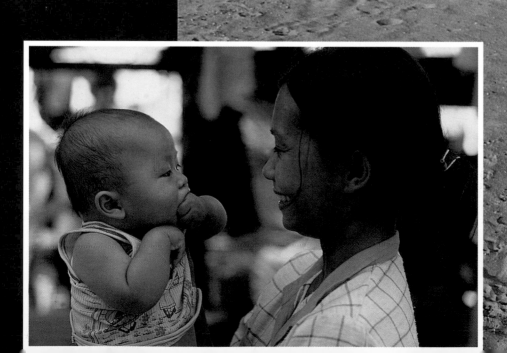

Below: The remains of one small boat that washed up on the shores of Thailand.
Inset: A mother plays with her child at the Songkla refugee camp in Thailand.

Conditions at the Songkla camp were crowded and harsh.

New refugees were arriving on Thailand's shores every day. There were so many boat people that officials could not fit them all into the camp. On the beach, there were hundreds of crying children. One pregnant woman had malaria, a serious tropical disease. She was so sick, she didn't even know the name of the country she was in. In a few days, she would give birth there.

In the middle of the night, a friend woke me up at my hotel. He'd recently been to the beach, and discovered that the woman had gone into labor.

My friend and I ran down the beach, picked up the woman and snuck her—past the guards—into the camp. We brought her to a doctor, and explained everything. At 2:30 in the morning, she gave birth to a beautiful girl.

As the sun rose over the water one day, the woman told me her story. It had been illegal to leave Vietnam. But, if a person paid a large amount of money to a gangster, passage could secretly be arranged on one of the boats. This woman's husband could afford to pay for only one person to leave. He decided that he would stay in Vietnam and his wife would flee the country.

"I'll probably never see my husband again," she told me. "But I'll never stop loving him. He's such a brave man. He decided to stay behind, so my baby and I would have a chance to be free someplace else."

A mother rests after giving birth to a baby girl at the Songkla camp in Thailand.

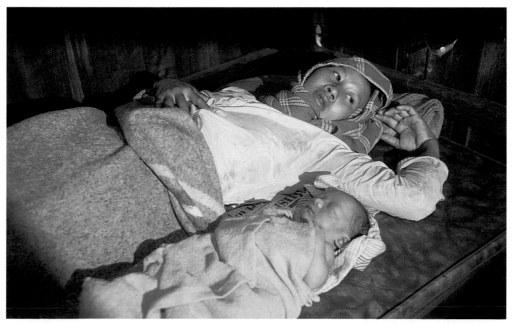

From Thailand, I traveled to the Palau Bidong refugee camp in Malaysia. The Palau Bidong camp was actually located on an island, cut off from the rest of Malaysia. I had to take a boat there. From the water, the shoreline looked as if it were covered with some type of brown mass.

As the boat got closer, the brown mass started to move. When I finally arrived, I realized that I'd been looking at some of the camp's 36,000 refugees. They were all jammed closely together and waited on the beach to see if the boat was bringing them food.

Right: The refugee camp at Palau Bidong, Malaysia, was packed with more than 36,000 hungry people.
Inset: Two youngsters play with a model boat they made from soda cans.

The Palau Bidong camp was a dreary place. Piles of garbage were everywhere. And there were no sewers. I'd been warned a number of times not to drink the water because it wasn't clean.

I got my best advice from a refugee boy about 12 years old.

"You journalists come here from all over the world," he said. "You take a bunch of pictures, and your boat's still waiting for you. Then you go back home after a half hour, and we're left, sitting and sitting and sitting. The only way to tell our story is if you stay here a while."

Barbed wire kept refugee children inside the Palau Bidong camp.

I had to agree with him. For several days, I remained on the island, sleeping in my clothes. I took pictures, and talked with the people. In the camp, everyone was dirty and poor. But once I sat down with a person and had a conversation, I realized that he or she had been a doctor, professor, or financial expert in Vietnam.

The boy told me, "If you're a Vietnamese refugee, there are two happy days in your life. The first is when you leave Vietnam. That's when you say goodbye to war and killing. The second is when you get out of this camp—and go to another country, where you can finally live in peace."

Aside from the dirt and poverty, life on the island was also extremely boring. The young boy, however, decided to spend his time there wisely. He was going to learn English, he told me. He asked every journalist who visited the camp to give him American books and magazines.

Opposite: A doctor offers medical help to a sick refugee at Palau Bidong.

I gave this child my address and phone number, but never expected to hear from him again. A year and a half later, I was home in New York, reading the newspaper on a Sunday morning, when the phone rang.

"Remember me?" the boy on the line asked.

He'd taught himself English, and his family had been accepted into Canada. He loved school, and had recently gotten a new bicycle. His father had a good job, and the family was the happiest they had ever been. It filled me with hope to hear that at least one family found happiness after this experience.

Left and opposite: Despite their suffering, many refugee children have been able to find happiness after leaving Vietnam.

The year I visited the refugee camps, China invaded Vietnam again. Vietnam's Chinese citizens—who had lived in the country for centuries—now found themselves distrusted by their neighbors. Many joined the waves of other Vietnamese boat people.

I met some of these ethnic Chinese refugees during a later visit to Hong Kong. Some were still stuck on boats, waiting at the docks while officials debated whether or not to admit them to the camps.

The boats of newly arrived Vietnamese refugees crowd Hong Kong harbor.

But Hong Kong was not large enough to hold all the people who wanted to live there. The territory— a British colony that was scheduled to be turned over to China in 1997—is only 415 square miles in area. In 1995, more than 5.5 million people were crammed into that small space.

By then, 20,900 refugees were left in Hong Kong—out of 40,000 boat people worldwide who were still living in refugee camps. When the economy of Vietnam improved, 70,000 boat people went back to their country. Most did so voluntarily. But Hong Kong also forced some Vietnamese to leave.

The tale of the boat people had many happy endings. Refugees were eventually accepted in 34 countries.

Refugees crowd together behind a fence at a holding station in Hong Kong.

Refugees cheer upon hearing of their acceptance to a new country as permanent citizens.

When I remember the boat people, I think of their extraordinary bravery. In the hope of freedom, they put themselves in the greatest danger possible. I also think of the excitement I saw when the refugees were told that they were approved to be citizens of other countries. During their official ceremonies, parents and children stood together, glowing, as they raised their arms to take an oath of allegiance to their new country. Finally, it seemed, the bad times were behind them. And the future was full of promise.

FURTHER READING

Barr, Roger. *The Vietnam War*. San Diego, CA: Lucent, 1991.

Devaney, John. *The Vietnam War*. Danbury, CT: Watts, 1993.

Gareth Stevens, eds. *Vietnam Is My Home*. Milwaukee, WI: Gareth Stevens, 1992.

Jacobsen, Karen. *Vietnam*. Danbury, CT: Children's Press, 1992.

INDEX

PHOTO CREDITS